THE STORY BEHIND
GROUNDHOG DAY

JACK READER

PowerKiDS
press™

New York

Published in 2020 by The Rosen Publishing Group, Inc.
29 East 21st Street, New York, NY 10010

First Edition

Editor: Tanya Dellaccio
Book Design: Reann Nye

Photo Credits: Cover, p. 1 Jeff Swensen/Getty Images News/Getty Images; pp. 4, 6, 8, 10, 12, 14, 16, 18, 20, 22 (background) Preto Perola/Shutterstock.com; p. 5 ElenaZet/Shutterstock.com; p. 7 Paul Reeves Photography/Shutterstock.com; p. 9 gresei/Shutterstock.com; p. 11 Donat Sorokin/Getty Images; p. 13 zlikovec/Shutterstock.com; p. 15 Coatesy/Shutterstock.com; pp. 17, 22 Alex Wong/Getty Images News/Getty Images; p. 19 Archie Carpenter/Getty Images News/Getty Images; p. 21 Chris Hondros/Getty Images News/Getty Images.

Cataloging-in-Publication Data

Names: Reader, Jack.
Title: The story behind Groundhog Day / Jack Reader.
Description: New York : PowerKids Press, 2020. | Series: Holiday histories | Includes glossary and index.
Identifiers: ISBN 9781725300446 (pbk.) | ISBN 9781725300460 (library bound) | ISBN 9781725300453 (6pack)
Subjects: LCSH: Groundhog Day–Juvenile literature.
Classification: LCC GT4995.G76 R29 2020 | DDC 394.261–dc23
Manufactured in the United States of America

CPSIA Compliance Information: Batch #CSPK19. For Further Information contact Rosen Publishing, New York, New York at 1-800-237-9932.

CONTENTS

Winter or Spring?

Is spring right around the corner or will there be six more weeks of winter? People in the United States and Canada ask this each year on February 2. But they don't ask a **meteorologist**—they ask a groundhog! Groundhog Day has been **celebrated** for over 130 years.

Hiding Until Spring

Groundhogs live in forests and meadows in North America, which is where Groundhog Day is celebrated today. During the winter, groundhogs **hibernate** in their **burrows** for months without moving or eating. They come out in the springtime when the weather gets warmer.

An Important Day

February 2 is about halfway between the first day of winter and the first day of spring. An ancient **Celtic** holiday called Imbolc falls on this day. Imbolc celebrates the end of winter and the beginning of spring. Ancient Egyptians and Babylonians likely celebrated a similar holiday.

Candlemas

As Christianity spread throughout Europe, Imbolc turned into a new holiday called Candlemas. Christians celebrated important figures on February 2 by lighting candles. Some people believed there would be 40 more days of winter if it was sunny on Candlemas.

Turning to Animals

People across Europe looked for animals coming out of hibernation on Candlemas. Some looked for bears, while others looked for smaller burrowing animals. They believed this was a way to tell if the weather was getting warmer, or if it was going to continue being colder.

13

Watching animals to learn about changes in the weather was common in Germany. Some Germans believed if a badger came out of its burrow on a sunny day and saw its shadow, more winter weather was on its way. If it didn't see its shadow, spring was coming soon.

The First Celebration

In the 18th and 19th centuries, many German **immigrants** moved to North America and settled in Pennsylvania. They turned to groundhogs, which were common in the area, to **predict** the weather. The first official Groundhog Day celebration took place February 2, 1887, in Punxsutawney, Pennsylvania.

A group of businessmen and hunters known as the Punxsutawney Groundhog Club started the yearly celebration. They headed to a place called Gobbler's Knob to see if a groundhog named Punxsutawney Phil would see his shadow. He did, which meant six more weeks of winter!

GOBBLER'S KNOB

PHIL

The Holiday Today

Since the first Groundhog Day celebration in 1887, crowds have gathered every February 2 at Gobbler's Knob for Phil's prediction. A group called the Inner Circle runs the event. Members wear fancy hats and pretend to speak to Phil in groundhog language.

21

Trusting the Groundhog

Records show that Phil has only been right about 40 percent of the time when predicting the weather. Other areas in the United States and Canada also have weather-predicting groundhogs. Even though their predictions aren't always correct, Groundhog Day is still a fun celebration!

GLOSSARY

burrow: A hole an animal digs in the ground for shelter.

celebrate: To do something special or enjoyable for an important event or holiday.

Celtic: Having to do with a group of people, such as the Irish, who lived in ancient Britain and parts of western Europe.

hibernate: To sleep or rest all winter without waking up.

immigrant: A person who comes to a country to live there.

meteorologist: A scientist who studies the atmosphere and weather.

predict: To guess what will happen in the future based on facts or knowledge.

INDEX

WEBSITES

Due to the changing nature of Internet links, PowerKids Press has developed an online list of websites related to the subject of this book. This site is updated regularly. Please use this link to access the list: www.powerkidslinks.com/HH/groundhog